RYA Start P

Technical Editor Paul Mara

2nd edition 2009
Reprinted February 2011, May 2011, October 2011
April 2012, January 2013, July 2013, November 2013
May 2014, December 2014, March 2015, June 2015
February 2016, July 2016, March 2017, August 2017, March 2018
August 2018, February 2019, June 2019, August 2019, March 2020

© Jon Mendez
First Published 2006
This Edition 2009
The Royal Yachting Association
RYA House, Ensign Way, Hamble,
Southampton SO31 4YA
Tel: 02380 604 100
Web: www.rya.org.uk
Follow us on Twitter @RYAPublications
or on YouTube

We welcome feedback on our
publications at publications@rya.org.uk

You can check content updates for RYA
Publications at
www.rya.org.uk/go/bookschangelog

ISBN: 9781906435479
RYA Order Code: G48

All rights reserved. No part of this publication may be reproduced,
stored in a retrieval system, or transmitted, in any form or by any
means, electronic, mechanical, photocopying, recording or otherwise,
without the prior permission in writing of the publishers.

A CIP record of this book is available from the British Library

Note: While all reasonable care has been taken in the preparation
of this book, the publisher takes no responsibility for the use of the
methods or products or contracts described in the book.

Cover Design: Pete Galvin
Photographic credits: McMurdo, Piplers of Poole, Garmin, Icom,
RNLI, Jon Mendez, PPL, Paul Mara, Laurence West, Seaward
Marine, Bisham Abbey School of Navigation, Scorpion RIBs, Paul
Glatzel and Musto.
Typeset: Creativebyte
Proofreading and glossary: Alan Thatcher
Printed in China through World Print

Sustainable Forests

Contents

How to Start Powerboating

For many people the chance to go out on the water and try a boat starts with a trip on a friend's boat, most first time powerboaters come back hooked and want more! A RYA powerboat training course allows you the best of both worlds – your chance to drive someone else's boat and the opportunity to gain the experience and knowledge to be safe afloat. More importantly you will come away understanding how boats work, the equipment you will need and the type, style and design features that you would want on your boat should you decide to purchase one.

If you are lucky enough to already own a boat the knowledge you gain will enable you to use your boat safely, to handle it more confidently and to really enjoy the sport.

This book is designed to accompany the RYA Powerboat courses:
Level 1 Start Powerboating
Level 2 Powerboat Handling
Level 2 is the recognised minimum standard for powerboat skippers.

If you hold Level 2 Powerboat Handling and are a British passport holder or British resident you are eligible for an International Certificate of Competence for power craft up to 10m in length.

Personal Buoyancy and Clothing

Before you consider going afloat you need to make a list of personal equipment you will use. The most important item will be your choice of either lifejackets or buoyancy aids for yourself and your crew.

Lifejackets are designed to turn an unconscious casualty in the water face up. Most are powered by a small gas canister which can be activated automatically when it comes in contact with the water. Automatic ones are especially good for children and those who are not confident in the water.

A buoyancy aid provides some buoyancy but not as much as a lifejacket and will not turn an unconscious person face up. However it will support a conscious swimmer. They are ideal for sports where you get very wet, are a good swimmer and are confident in the water. An automatic lifejacket is the best option if you are alone on a boat. Wear a lifejacket or buoyancy aid unless you are sure you don't need to.

Outer Clothing
There is a vast array of clothing available to suit all budgets and weather conditions, here are some examples.

Hot weather
Even when it is very hot you will need a minimum of a top, shorts, suitable footwear and don't forget a hat and plenty of sun cream. Remember to take a wind/waterproof jacket; when the sun goes in it soon gets very chilly.

Cool weather

More substantial windproof and waterproof clothing and boots are required, preferably with breathable under-layers.

Cold and extreme weather

When out on the water in cold weather or for long periods it is well worth the investment in buying a dry suit. Fitted with special seals to keep the water out they can be worn over normal clothing or breathable layers. Excellent also if you are a safety boat crew because they allow you to enter the water and stay dry. Some people who expect to get wet prefer a wetsuit.

Other items to consider taking are hats, sunglasses, sun cream, goggles, drinks, water, snack foods, medication (including anti-seasickness pills or bands) and a towel.

Parts of the Boat

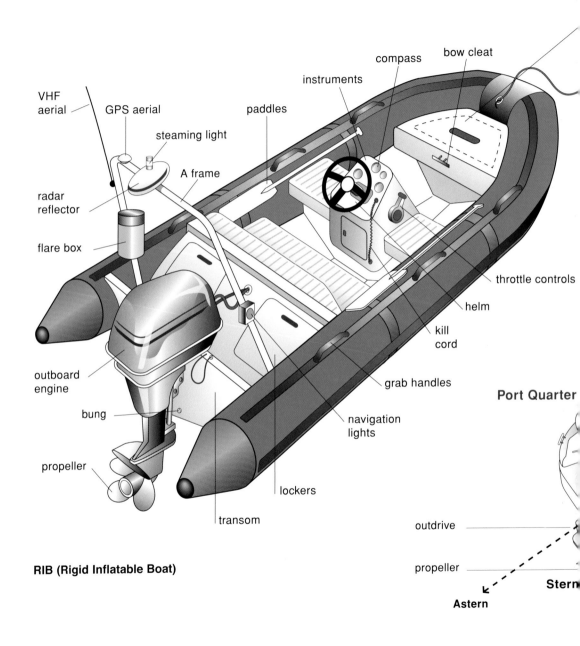

VHF aerial

GPS aerial

steaming light

A frame

radar reflector

flare box

outboard engine

bung

propeller

paddles

instruments

compass

bow cleat

throttle controls

helm

kill cord

grab handles

navigation lights

lockers

transom

RIB (Rigid Inflatable Boat)

Port Quarter

outdrive

propeller

Stern

Astern

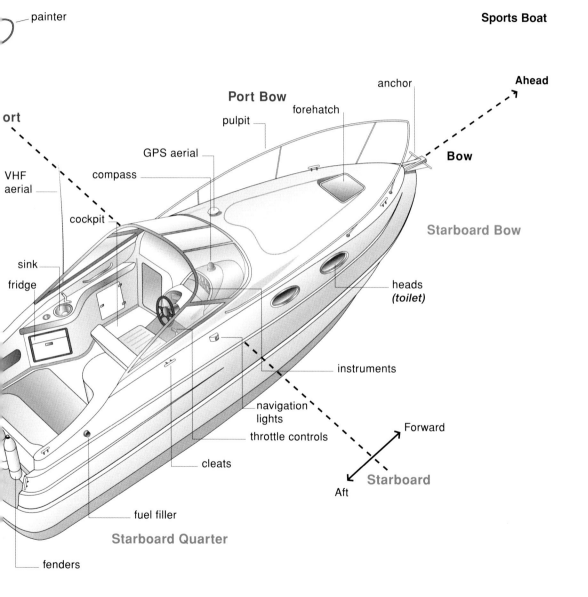

anchor locker

painter

Sports Boat

Ahead

anchor

Port Bow

forehatch

ort

pulpit

Bow

GPS aerial

VHF
aerial

compass

Starboard Bow

cockpit

sink

heads
(toilet)

fridge

instruments

navigation
lights

Forward

throttle controls

cleats

Starboard

Aft

fuel filler

Starboard Quarter

fenders

Types of Craft

There are many different types and sizes of small powered boats available, below is a selection of the most popular.

RIB (Rigid Inflatable Boat)

Vee hull with inflatable tubes for buoyancy and stability. Tubes also cushion the ride when it is rough, however this creates less internal volume as tubes take up space. Good rescue boat but now also popular as a family and fishing boat. A well-designed and driven RIB can handle seas far in excess of those handled by other comparable sized boats. Usually fitted with outboard engines, some larger boats are fitted with inboard engines.

Sports Boat

Good all round family craft in flat to slight seas. Better internal volume than a RIB, but ultimately poorer sea keeping and usually drier. Available with outboard or inboard engines. Many people start their boating with this style of boat.

Both RIBs and sports boats have a planing hull, this can be shallow or deep Vee. Shallow Vees plane easily and give a flatter wake but slam more in poor sea conditions. Flatter panels aft allow the hull to skim across the surface. A deep Vee gives a smooth ride in rougher water but requires more power to propel it.

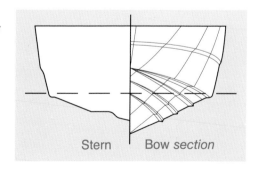

Stern | Bow *section*

Displacement Hull
The classic fishing hull and more rounded (duck shape). Works by pushing water out of the way as they move. Good sea boats but are slow and inclined to roll.

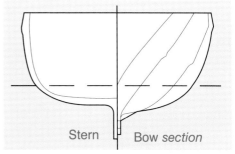

Semi-Displacement Hull
Combines some of the features of both the displacement and the Vee hull. Good sea keeping with moderate speed. Needs a lot of power to go fast, so can use a lot of fuel.

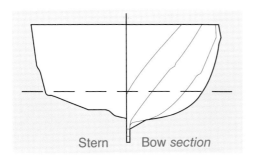

Dory or Cathedral Hull
Stable with an open deck, good load carrying capacity, low power will make it plane. Hard ride in choppy water.

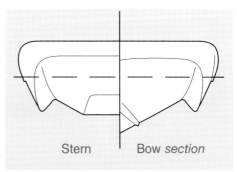

Engines and Drives

Small boats are powered by several different types of engine and drive systems. For small planing craft the outboard is still the most popular engine especially since the newest outboards are so much quieter, lighter and economical. The propeller is still the most popular way to transmit engine power to the water.

Drive Types

Inboard engine with shaft drive

Engine is within the hull and drives a gearbox and shaft. The shaft passes through the hull on a fitting called a stern gland making a watertight seal. Steering is achieved with a rudder. A simple system that is reliable and generally low maintenance.

An Outdrive or Stern drive

Engine is within the hull but this time it drives an outdrive on the back of the hull. While steering the unit pivots from side to side and can be tilted enabling it to travel through shallow water. However this system means that there are lots of mechanical parts in the water all the time.

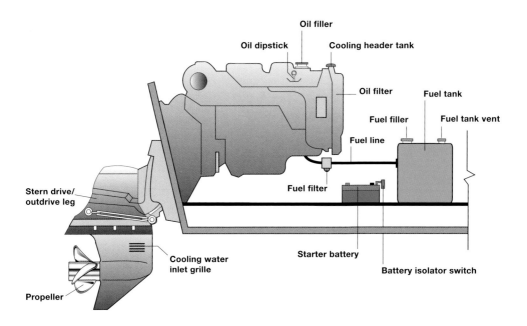

Outboard

Whole engine and drive train are carried on the stern of the boat. A self-contained unit that pivots and tilts just like an outdrive, but has the benefit that the drive can be tilted clear of the water when not in use. Smaller ones are tiller steered and can be stolen. Larger ones usually have wheel steering and a seated driving position.

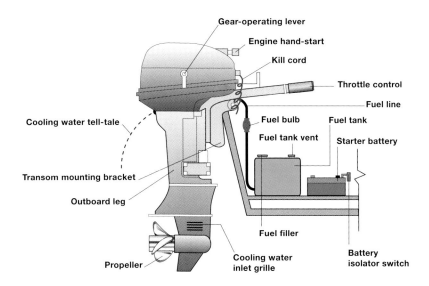

Jet drive

High volume pump (impellor) sucks water from under the boat. It is squirted out of a movable nozzle at the stern. This provides steering and with the aid of a clam cover, reverse gear. They are great for shallow water but can lose power in rougher weather due to the pump inlet lifting out of the water.

Boat Controls

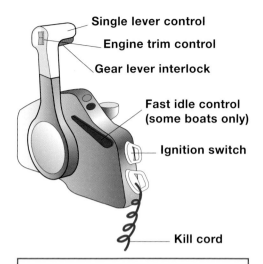

Single lever control

Engine trim control

Gear lever interlock

Fast idle control (some boats only)

Ignition switch

Kill cord

Most powerboats have a single lever control with neutral in the centre, pushing the lever forward engages ahead gear, pulling it backwards gives astern gear. Pushing the lever further in either direction increases the revolutions and hence the speed. Many tiller steered craft have a twist grip throttle on the tiller arm and a separate gear lever on the side of the engine. The latest have a combined gear / throttle on the hand grip. The trim control is used to raise and lower the leg. It also allows the drive angle to be optimised for sea conditions and loading.

Before Starting

Check that it is not in gear and the propeller is clear. Start whilst in neutral. Some engines need either choke or extra revs to start. When it starts, check the cooling water is exiting. Use the gear lever interlock correctly; you need to squeeze it to engage gear. Release after each engagement of gears. Always allow a pause in neutral when moving from ahead to astern gear. Use a solid push to put the craft into gear, without dragging of the gears. Check that the steering operates smoothly from lock to lock and without the need for excessive effort. Turn the wheel in the direction you wish the boat to move. Always steer before engaging gear. It is best practice to use one hand for the steering and one for the gears (throttle). This is especially important at higher speed. Tiller steered boats require you to push or pull the tiller in the opposite direction to the direction you want to go.

Kill Cord

The Kill cord is very important. It's there for everyone's safety. Its purpose is to stop the engine if you move away from the helm, or fall out. It also stops the boat running away and injuring you or others. Always check that the kill cord works. Attach it to yourself preferably around the leg, EVERY time that you go boating.

Operating at Planing Speed

When intending to travel at higher speeds, you must keep a really good all-round look-out. Check it is clear before you turn, be aware of other water users and the effect of your wash. Load and trim the boat according to the conditions and don't go boating when it is beyond your or your boat's abilities. Operators of craft with more powerful engines should make themselves aware of the handling characteristics of these craft and consider undertaking training appropriate to these boats. The RYA Intermediate and Advanced courses will prepare you for faster and more powerful craft. Ensure all crew are appropriately seated with secure handholds before setting off. When operating at speed, be aware that the motion in the forward end of the boat will be more noticeable than it will be further aft. In general, and subject to the boat being trimmed appropriately, passengers will have a safer and more comfortable ride when seated aft rather than forward.

Crew and Rope Work

Your crew are your best asset on the boat, with a well trained crew your boating will be far safer and enjoyable. Teach them to throw a line, tie a few simple knots and how to cleat off.

Round Turn and Two Half Hitches - Easy to tie and can be undone whilst under load.

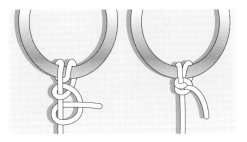

Clove Hitch - Good for fenders and light loads, can work loose.

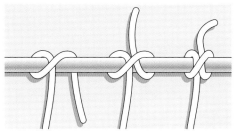

Sheet Bend - Good for joining two lines, especially if they are different diameters. Can only be undone without a load on.

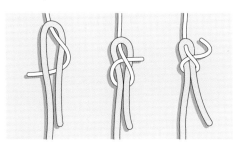

Cleating Off - Take a complete turn around the cleat, then follow this with two figures of eight, finish with a complete turn.

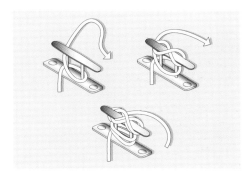

Bowline - The most used knot in boating, good for mooring lines. Will take a great load and can still be released. Can only be undone when there is no load.

Trailing and Launching

Trailing your boat allows you to explore many other boating areas. It can also reduce your boating costs, because you do not have to pay marina fees, although some harbour authorities do charge to launch a boat. The laws on trailing can be complicated: check with the RYA (www.rya.org.uk) or your national highways agency websites for full details. Practise driving a car with a trailer; remember that the whole unit is much larger than just a car and will require extra room to manoeuvre. Allow more time when you need to brake.

On arrival at your launch site you need to allow the wheel bearings on the trailer to cool before you launch, cold sea water can seep past the bearing seals and cause corrosion. Whilst waiting you can assess the launch area and slipway, noting how steep it is and any obstructions or other hazards. Be aware as to the length of the slipway and how it ends. You will also need to find secure parking for the trailer and tow vehicle. Many of the items, which need to be considered for launching, can be prepared beforehand, e.g. weather forecasts, tidal information, ownership of the slipway, permission to launch or harbour dues.

Pre-launch checks
Remove trailer board straps and cover, insert bung and check the boat, engine and propeller for damage, load the boat with equipment and supplies. If running water is available you can start and pre-warm the engine using the muffs.

Launching
Aim to float the boat off the trailer; you may need a long rope or a bar to keep the tow vehicle out of the water. When it is afloat release the winch strap and push the boat off or start the engine with it partially raised and reverse it clear. Now either get your crew to hold the boat in the deeper water or move it to a pontoon making sure that the tow vehicle and trailer are parked well clear of the slipway.

Recovery

This is a reversal of the launch process; however it is essential that nobody gets between the boat and the shore (especially if on a lee shore) or trailer. Remember to raise the engine on the approach but keep the cooling water circulating. Unwind the winch strap keeping hands clear of the winch handle. Attach the winch strap and ideally a second line before you pull it clear of the water. Flush the engine through at the earliest opportunity.

Before Towing

Ensure the boat is fully secure on the trailer. Use tie-down straps on the D-rings on the transom to hold the rear of the boat to the trailer. Connect the D-ring on the bow to hold the front of the boat in position. Use a safety chain between the vehicle and the trailer in case the two become separated. Re-attach the trailer board, check that the lights work and off you go.

Boat Handling

Some points to consider when handling a boat: How much **windage** it has, how the **stream** affects it, how much **momentum** it has, is there any **prop effect**, where does it **pivot** and how is it **steered**?

The Natural Elements

Windage

Vessel A has much greater areas exposed to the wind than B - this means that its windage is higher; this must be taken into account when handling the boat especially in a marina environment.

Stream

Stream like windage affects all craft in different ways, a displacement craft (B) with a keel will be more affected by stream than windage, but the high sided small cruiser (A) with a planing hull will be more affected by wind than stream.

Your Boat's Characteristics

Momentum - Carrying way & stopping

Unfortunately boats don't have brakes so you need to learn to use neutral and to be able to assess how quickly it will stop. Good boat handlers spend a lot of time in neutral just letting the vessel move under its own momentum. All craft when put into neutral will keep moving until the momentum has been lost; this is called 'carrying way'. A large heavy vessel will require more power to make it move in the first place, hence when moving it has greater momentum and will keep moving longer when in neutral.

Sometimes you may need to use a small amount of engine power to halt the last of this momentum; however it's best to use nature's brakes - the wind and stream.

Because of the combination of wind, stream, and its handling characteristics, a boat is often travelling because of all of these forces. Especially at slow speed it is important to realise that the boat is often not travelling in the direction it is pointing (its heading).

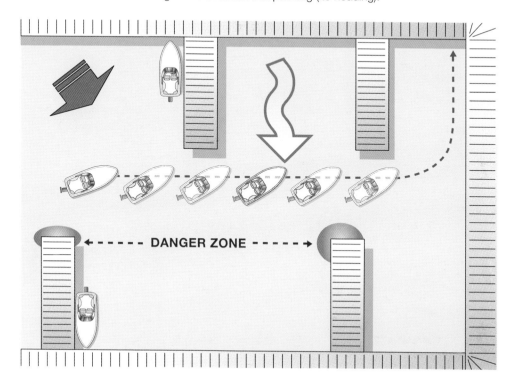

Wind or stream will be trying to move your craft downwind or downstream, therefore it is best to think of all areas downwind or downstream as your 'Danger Zone'. By knowing which direction stream and wind are trying to take the boat you can use them to your advantage, as nature's brakes to slow you or to assist you onto a berth. Learning how to read the elements and use them to your advantage is one of the key factors in stress-free boating.

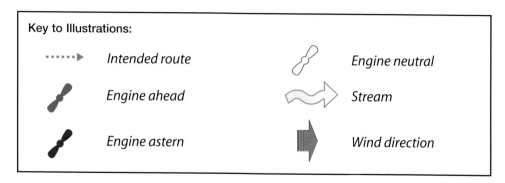

Prop Effect

When the engine is put into gear and the propeller turns it provides forward thrust, because of this rotation it also tries to move the stern to one side due to the paddle wheel or 'prop' effect. This affects shaft drive boats more than outboard or sterndrives, in "duoprops" it is almost non-existent. A right handed prop, i.e. one that turns to the right when viewed from behind, in ahead gear tries to walk the stern to the right (starboard). Conversely in astern it tries to walk the stern to the left (port). It is usual for this to be more noticeable in astern gear. If you know what a boat's propeller rotation is you can put this effect to good use when turning and berthing.

RIGHT HAND PROP AHEAD

RIGHT HAND PROP ASTERN

Pivot Points

Boats when going ahead steer from the stern, the pivot point is about one third back from the bow and when you put the wheel hard over to the left (port) and engage ahead gear, roughly one third of the vessel turns to port and the remainder goes to starboard.

When going astern the pivot point moves aft and when the wheel is hard over to the left (port) with astern gear engaged, one third of the vessel moves to port, the remainder to starboard.

All boats pivot at slightly different points, knowing where the pivot point is on your boat is one of the most important factors in all boat handling exercises.

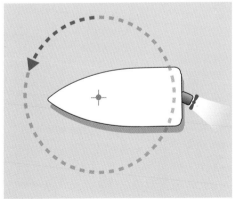

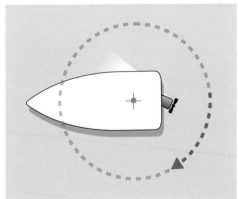

Ahead   **Astern**

Steering

The rudder works by deflecting water passing over it, because it is behind the propeller the effect is much greater when the propeller is turning. At slow speeds a 'burst of power' is very effective as it dramatically increases the water over the rudder without increasing too much speed.

Outboards and outdrives do not have rudders, they steer by squirting the water in the direction that the drive is turned, as this only happens when it is in gear you need to think 'no gear – no steer'. Because you want the drive in the correct direction before power is applied remember 'wheel before gear'.

Turning

Steering on boats is not the same as on cars so when turning in a small space you need to take into account all the points above.

Shaft Drive

Position the boat roughly in the centre of the space taking into account wind and stream. Approach as slowly as possible, speed carried into the turn will make the turn larger. Turn in the direction that the astern prop effect will assist. Wheel hard over and give a burst ahead, engage neutral. As the rate of turn slows or if space is short give a burst astern; changes in rudder position will have no effect because there is not enough room to gain steerageway. Momentum and prop walk are now turning the boat. Keep this process going until the correct direction is achieved, then select ahead and drive away.

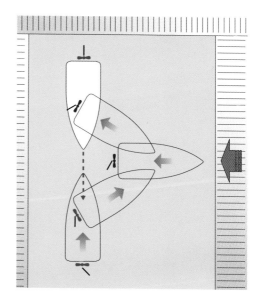

Turning an Outdrive or Outboard

Position yourself as for the previous manoeuvre then to turn - wheel hard over to starboard. Engage ahead. Monitor the turn. Neutral when space is short. Wheel hard over to port. Engage astern. Monitor the turn. Neutral when space is short. Straighten wheel, engage ahead and drive out.

It is usual to turn into whichever element is strongest, either wind or stream.

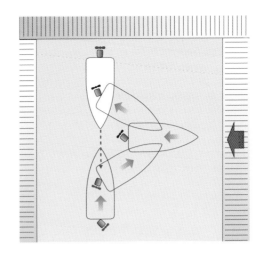

Coming Alongside

Outboards and Outdrives

Successful manoeuvring between pontoons and other boats is easier if you take account of how your craft reacts. Check what the wind and stream are doing and what effect it will have on your boat and manoeuvre. Approaching into the wind or stream means they can act as a brake. Ideally try to approach using whichever will have the greatest effect. Brief your crew so they know exactly what is expected of them. Prepare fenders and lines. Plan your 'escape' route, just in case the manoeuvre goes wrong.

Start your approach as far off the pontoon as is practical. Your angle of approach should be about 30°–40°. Use neutral to keep speed and momentum low. When you are about a boat's length away, steer away from the pontoon and give a touch ahead. This will straighten the boat, try to let the boat stop without using astern. If you are too fast or too steep to the pontoon, steer towards the pontoon and engage astern gear momentarily to bring the boat alongside. This has the effect of slowing you and bringing the stern in. Look sideways to be sure that the boat is stationary.

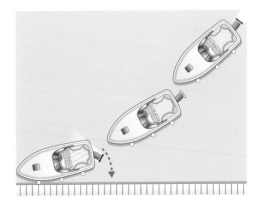

Shaft Drive

Plan so that you use prop effect to aid berthing. Approach slowly at about 30°. Control speed with neutral and use the rudder to continue steering. As the boat glides alongside engage astern, this will slow the boat and prop effect will pull the stern in. Look sideways to ensure that the boat is stationary. A centre line is very useful to hold a boat on a mooring whilst you sort out the correct mooring lines.

When wind or stream are making the manoeuvre difficult you will need to be more positive and can also use lines to assist especially on an outboard or outdrive. Motor up to the berth and attach a bow line. Turn the wheel towards the pontoon, engage astern at tick over. The craft will be pulled alongside.

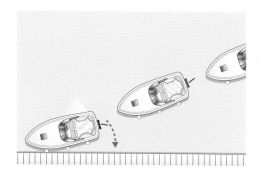

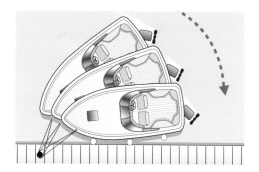

Leaving

Leaving a pontoon can be a very simple manoeuvre. If the route ahead is clear and there is no wind or stream a good push off the pontoon and driving away in ahead could suffice. However it is usually better to come away in reverse utilising the shape of the boat to roll the bow in first.

Outboard or Outdrive

Fender the bow, steer towards the pontoon, engage ahead briefly, into neutral, then steer away from the pontoon. Engage reverse and as the stern comes away, straighten up the wheel. Once well clear move off ahead.

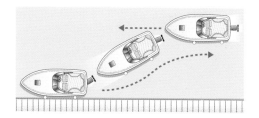

To leave with any wind or stream element holding you on, you may need lines. Decide if you want to leave ahead or astern.

Outboards or Outdrives

To leave astern – rig a bow line as a slip line and fender the bow area. Turn the wheel away from the dock and engage astern, as the stern comes clear, engage neutral, slip the line and reverse away.

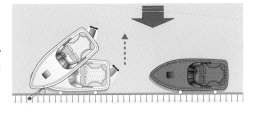

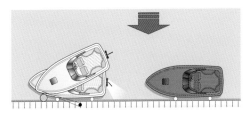

Shaft Drive

To leave astern – rig a bow spring as a slip line and fender the bow area. Turn the wheel towards the dock and engage ahead, as the spring tightens this will force the stern out. Engage neutral, slip the line and reverse away.

To leave ahead – all types, rig a stern spring as a slip line. Fender the stern well and engage astern.

As the spring tightens it forces the bow out. Engage neutral, slip the spring and motor away.

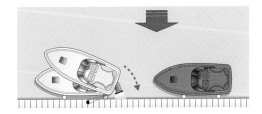

Securing the Boat
Some small boats are secured with just a single line called the painter (bow line); larger craft may use up to four lines. The bow line (painter) holds the bow to the pontoon and should go forward of the boat. The stern line holds the stern to the pontoon, it should go aft of the boat. The fore (bow) spring stops the boat moving forwards. The aft (stern) spring stops the boat moving backwards.

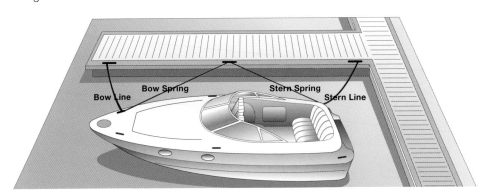

Mooring Buoys

Mooring buoys are provided by harbour authorities and clubs, some for short stay (temporary) mooring, others are for longer periods and usually cost less than a pontoon mooring.

To Pick up a Mooring Buoy

Make sure you know which part of the buoy to make fast to. Watch out for trailing lines on the down-stream side. Tell your crew your intentions, prepare a line early, you may need to use a boat hook. Before you start, plan your escape route. If wind and stream are together approach into them, they will help slow you down. Keep your speed slow, using neutral to control it. Remember to look sideways to help judge your speed. Turn the boat slightly at the last moment to bring the buoy in on the bow area. If wind is against the stream, judge which is the stronger, approach into it, remember you may need to use astern to stop. If using your line to tie off, put at least two turns around the ring to reduce chafe. When using the pick up buoy ensure that you also attach a secure line to the ring.

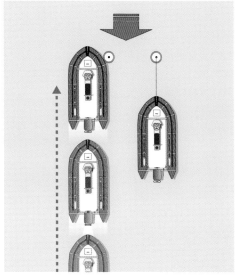

In boats that have high windage or poor bow access, it is often easier to approach stern to the elements. Rig a long line from a bow cleat to the cockpit area. Gently reverse up to the buoy. The long bow line led aft will allow you to tie on as before and the boat will gently swing around, for short stays you can use just a stern line.

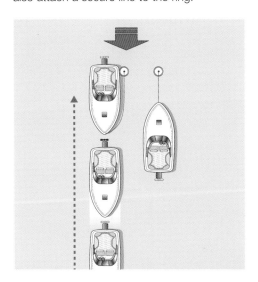

Anchoring

There are a variety of anchors for small boats, all work well provided that there is enough chain and rope out (scope) for the depth of water. The amount is different when using rope & chain than all chain. An anchor works by having a horizontal pull. On a rope / chain combination the chain acts as a shock absorber, adds weight and reduces chafe.

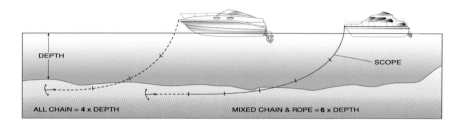

DEPTH

SCOPE

ALL CHAIN = **4 x DEPTH**

MIXED CHAIN & ROPE = **6 x DEPTH**

Anchoring is similar to approaching a mooring but without a fixed target. A boat with an open bow area makes it much easier and going forward is simple. On boats with a high foredeck keep one hand holding on at all times.

Choosing your spot
Look for shelter for the duration of your stay. Check the chart for the suitability of the bottom. Consider the rise and fall of the tide, will there be enough water later? How are other craft anchored – will there be enough room to swing? Prepare the anchor and chain / rope for the depth early, secure the end to the boat. Approach as for a mooring, once the boat is stopped lower the anchor to the seabed. Let the wind and stream drift the boat back from the anchor, you may need gentle astern power while your crew feeds out the scope. Check it is holding by engaging astern briefly to dig the anchor in. Use two objects in line with each other (a transit) ahead and to the side to check you are stationary. If the anchor is dragging raise it and start again. When leaving an anchorage, engage ahead briefly to ease the load, haul in the warp, taking care not to run over your line. Stow the anchor securely.

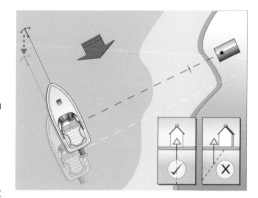

Collision Regulations

A skipper's decisions as to what action to take at sea are governed by the International Rules for the Prevention of Collisions at Sea (IRPCS). A great deal of the Rules are common sense; for example, you have a responsibility to obey the Rules, keep a good look out, use a safe speed, assess if there is a risk of collision and if so know what to do.

As a small power boat skipper you give way to all other craft. Other Rules to be aware of are:

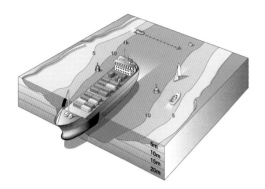

Narrow channels: Do not impede any vessel which requires the depth of water available in the narrow channel.

Sailing Vessels: Be aware of the Rules for sailing vessels.

When overtaking: Do not impede any vessel that you are overtaking.

In a head on situation: Both vessels shall alter course and turn to starboard.

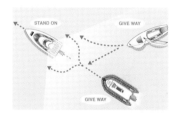

Crossing situations: Give way to traffic coming from the right.

Give way vessel: Take early substantial action.

Stand on vessel: Keep your course and speed BUT watch the other vessel; be prepared to take avoiding action.

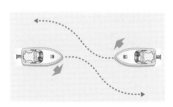

Remember at sea no vessel has automatic right of way.

The above Rules only apply to vessels in sight of one another. In poor visibility we are all give way vessels.

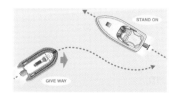

Day Shapes and Lights

By day displaying black shapes identifies a vessel's 'special conditions'. In poor visibility and at night vessels show lights to identify what they are, which direction they are travelling and if they have any special situations.

Fog signals

— One long blast (4-6 seconds)   o One short blast (2 seconds)

	At night	By day
A vessel under 7m and 7 knots. A single white light could also be a vessel at anchor or a vessel seen from astern.		
A powered vessel under 50m shows a white masthead light, a white sternlight and port and starboard lights. Fog — every two minutes.		
A powered craft over 50m displays two masthead white lights – the forward one lower than the one at the stern – a white sternlight and its port and starboard lights. Fog — every two minutes.		
A yacht under sail either shows a tricolour; or port and starboard lights plus a white sternlight. If the engine is used, it becomes a powered vessel and must display the appropriate lights. Its day shape when motor sailing is a cone pointing downward. Fog — o o every two minutes.		
At anchor under 50m only one white light is required. The day shape is a black ball. A vessel over 50m at anchor displays two white lights, with the one at the stern lower than the one at the bow. <100m Fog rapid ringing of bell for five seconds every minute. >100m Bell rung forward, gong aft for five seconds every minute.		
Code flag A indicates a vessel engaged in diving operations – keep well clear at slow speed.		

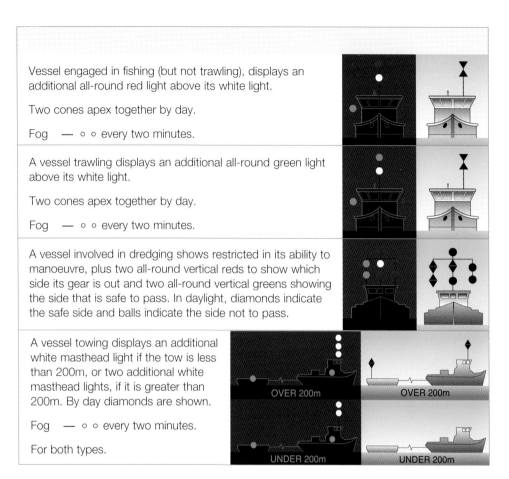

Vessel engaged in fishing (but not trawling), displays an additional all-round red light above its white light.

Two cones apex together by day.

Fog — ∘ ∘ every two minutes.

A vessel trawling displays an additional all-round green light above its white light.

Two cones apex together by day.

Fog — ∘ ∘ every two minutes.

A vessel involved in dredging shows restricted in its ability to manoeuvre, plus two all-round vertical reds to show which side its gear is out and two all-round vertical greens showing the side that is safe to pass. In daylight, diamonds indicate the safe side and balls indicate the side not to pass.

A vessel towing displays an additional white masthead light if the tow is less than 200m, or two additional white masthead lights, if it is greater than 200m. By day diamonds are shown.

Fog — ∘ ∘ every two minutes.

For both types.

OVER 200m

OVER 200m

UNDER 200m

UNDER 200m

Sounds can be used to indicate what a vessel is about to do. You should have the equipment to make them on board.

One short blast	○	"I am turning to starboard".
Two short blasts	○○	"I am turning to port".
Three short blasts	○○○	"My engines are going astern" – this does not necessarily mean the craft is going backwards.
Five or more short blasts	○○○○○	"I don't understand your intentions" – perhaps better known as "What on earth are you doing?"

Man Overboard

If Someone Goes Overboard

- Alert the rest of the crew by shouting 'Man overboard'.
- Instruct one person to point at the MOB at all times.
- At slow speed, continue straight until well clear of the MOB.
- Make a slow controlled turn towards the MOB ensuring you have enough room so as not to run them over.
- If you are in danger of running over the MOB, abandon the manoeuvre and start again.
- Your approach will be governed by the wind and is similar to that of approaching a mooring buoy (see page 23) without the stream element.

Approaching a MOB

There are two methods that work in Small Craft to recover a MOB:

Method One

Decide which side to pick up the casualty. On small boats this should be the opposite side to the controls. Start the approach from downwind. Slowly move the boat towards the casualty. Use neutral to manage your speed Aim to bring the MOB onto your windward bow. When the MOB is near, remove power and grab hold of the MOB. Switch off the engine*. Manhandle the MOB to an area of the boat where you can recover them.

Advantages

Good for craft with low freeboards. Allows waves to be taken head-on. Good if rough as MOB is unlikely to go under the boat.

Disadvantages

Can be difficult if you are alone. You can lose sight of the MOB under the bow. You will need to be very quick at collection time.

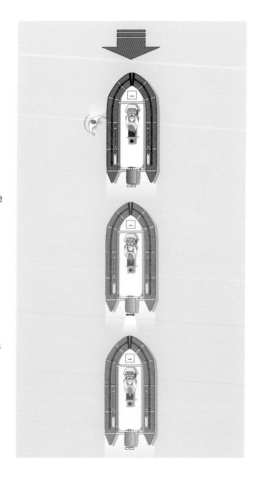

Method Two

This time go upwind of the MOB. Stop and position your boat beam on upwind of the MOB. Keep adjusting your position to drift down onto the MOB. When alongside switch off engine.*

Advantages

Suits high sided vessels where sight of the MOB is easily lost when approaching them into the wind. Provides some shelter to the MOB. Allows the boat to be brought alongside the MOB at the cockpit area where the freeboard is lowest. Bringing a MOB in on the leeward (downwind) side makes the boat lower in the water and so aids recovery.

Disadvantages

Can be uncomfortable being beam-on to the sea. Craft can be blown over the top of the MOB.

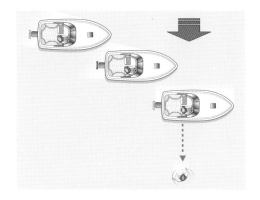

* As a skipper you need to balance the clear safety benefits of switching off the engine against the sea conditions and the location you are in. However, on RYA courses you will be expected to demonstrate best practice by switching the engine off. A MOB is a very serious situation, you should be prepared to call a MAYDAY if you have any doubt in your ability to recover the casualty.

Summoning Assistance

There are several ways that you can summon assistance to your boat; however you need first to assess how serious the problem is, and what help you require. If you, your boat or your crew are in immediate danger you must send out a Mayday call. This can be sent by a VHF (DSC) Mayday call, mobile phone, arm signals (if there are vessels close by), sounding your horn etc. or by using flares.

Mayday Call

How this is sent will depend slightly on the equipment; however the basic principles on a DSC radio are: remove the cover to the 'Distress' button, press and hold it for five seconds. This will broadcast a digital alert to all DSC equipped craft and the local coastguard. If properly programmed the alert will include your MMSI (a unique number identifying your craft) your position, the time and can also include the nature of the distress. You can follow up this DSC alert with a voice Mayday call as shown.

Mayday, Mayday, Mayday

This is powerboat Beta, Beta, Beta

Callsign MYFT6 MMSI 234001234

Mayday Beta

Callsign MYFT6 MMSI 234001234

My position is 50° 30'.5N, 001° 57'.5W

Have hit submerged object and am sinking

We require immediate assistance

Four persons on board

Abandoning to the life raft

Over

Now release the transmit button to receive a reply by voice. If you hear a Mayday do not use your radio unless you can offer assistance as you may mask vital transmissions. If you do not have a DSC radio use the voice procedure given above.

Mobile Phone

Mobiles can be used for requesting help, however they do have drawbacks, such as limited range in many coastal locations and only one person hears your call. Additionally, they cannot be homed in on as easily as a VHF transmission. A text message may stand a better chance of getting through.

Flares

Flares are an essential part of boating equipment; however there are several different types and you need to ensure you know how to use them before an emergency arises.

Recommended number to carry	Inshore	Sheltered waters
Red parachute flare The most effective long range flare; projects a bright flare to about 300m. Do not use near helicopters!	optional	0
Red hand-held flare Indicates precise position of craft, use when close to other craft or land.	3	2
Orange hand-held smoke Use in daylight, useful for attracting helicopter or lifeboat attention.	2	2

All flares are held and fired downwind and don't last forever, so check the expiry dates and dispose of old flares safely (see manufacturer's instructions).

For further guidance on distress signals visit the RYA website.

Fire

Many small boats are petrol powered, therefore it is sensible that you carry a fire extinguisher on board and you and your crew know how to use it. Most marine extinguishers use powder which is good at extinguishing electrical or flammable liquid fires. They work by smothering the fire, and therefore you must aim at the base of the fire. Fire blankets are also very good.

If you do not need urgent help e.g. you have run out of fuel and are not drifting into immediate danger your call for assistance can be made to another vessel or the coastguard.

Navigation

Charts

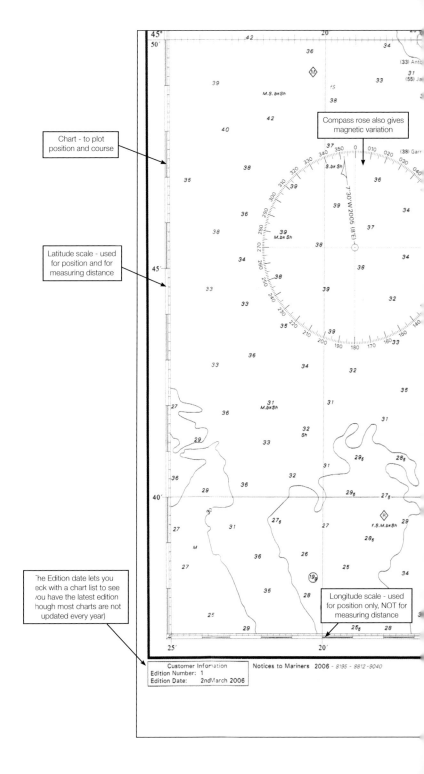

Chart - to plot position and course

Latitude scale - used for position and for measuring distance

Compass rose also gives magnetic variation

The Edition date lets you check with a chart list to see you have the latest edition (though most charts are not updated every year)

Longitude scale - used for position only, NOT for measuring distance

Customer Information
Edition Number: 1
Edition Date: 2nd March 2006

Notices to Mariners 2006 - *8195 - 8812-9040*

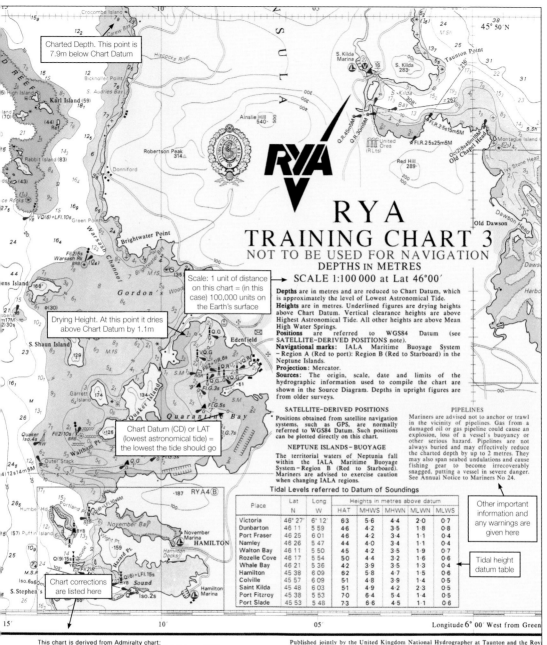

Charted Depth. This point is 7.9m below Chart Datum

Scale: 1 unit of distance on this chart = (in this case) 100,000 units on the Earth's surface

Drying Height. At this point it dries above Chart Datum by 1.1m

Chart Datum (CD) or LAT (lowest astronomical tide) = the lowest the tide should go

Other important information and any warnings are given here

Tidal height datum table

Chart corrections are listed here

RYA
TRAINING CHART 3
NOT TO BE USED FOR NAVIGATION
DEPTHS IN METRES
SCALE 1:100 000 at Lat 46°00´

Depths are in metres and are reduced to Chart Datum, which is approximately the level of Lowest Astronomical Tide.
Heights are in metres. Underlined figures are drying heights above Chart Datum. Vertical clearance heights are above Highest Astronomical Tide. All other heights are above Mean High Water Springs.
Positions are referred to WGS84 Datum (see SATELLITE–DERIVED POSITIONS note).
Navigational marks: IALA Maritime Buoyage System – Region A (Red to port): Region B (Red to Starboard) in the Neptune Islands.
Projection: Mercator.
Sources: The origin, scale, date and limits of the hydrographic information used to compile the chart are shown in the Source Diagram. Depths in upright figures are from older surveys.

SATELLITE–DERIVED POSITIONS
Positions obtained from satellite navigation systems, such as GPS, are normally referred to WGS84 Datum. Such positions can be plotted directly on this chart.

NEPTUNE ISLANDS – BUOYAGE
The territorial waters of Neptunia fall within the IALA Maritime Buoyage System – Region B (Red to Starboard). Mariners are advised to exercise caution when changing IALA regions.

PIPELINES
Mariners are advised not to anchor or trawl in the vicinity of pipelines. Gas from a damaged oil or gas pipeline could cause an explosion, loss of a vessel´s buoyancy or other serious hazard. Pipelines are not always buried and may effectively reduce the charted depth by up to 2 metres. They may also span seabed undulations and cause fishing gear to become irrecoverably snagged, putting a vessel in severe danger. See Annual Notice to Mariners No 24.

Tidal Levels referred to Datum of Soundings

Place	Lat N	Long W	Heights in metres above datum				
			HAT	MHWS	MHWN	MLWN	MLWS
Victoria	46° 27´	6° 12´	6·3	5·6	4·4	2·0	0·7
Dunbarton	46 11	5 59	4·6	4·2	3·5	1·8	0·8
Port Fraser	46 25	6 01	4·6	4·2	3·4	1·1	0·4
Namley	46 26	5 47	4·4	4·0	3·4	1·1	0·4
Walton Bay	46 11	5 50	4·5	4·2	3·5	1·9	0·7
Rozelle Cove	46 17	5 54	5·0	4·4	3·2	1·6	0·6
Whale Bay	46 21	5 36	4·2	3·9	3·5	1·3	0·4
Hamilton	45 38	6 09	6·2	5·8	4·7	1·5	0·6
Colville	45 57	6 09	5·1	4·8	3·9	1·4	0·5
Saint Kilda	45 48	6 03	5·1	4·9	4·2	2·3	0·5
Port Fitzroy	45 38	5 53	7·0	6·4	5·4	1·4	0·5
Port Slade	45 53	5 48	7·3	6·6	4·5	1·1	0·6

Longitude 6° 00´ West from Green

This chart is derived from Admiralty chart:
1652, corrected to New Edition Published 24th February 2005
2045, corrected to NM 1286/05

Published jointly by the United Kingdom National Hydrographer at Taunton and the Roy
www.ukho.gov.uk ☎ +44 (0)1823 337900
© RYA Copyright 2006

Position

Charts are the nautical equivalent of maps. The information they show allows you to navigate safely.

To define precise position on the Earth's surface two imaginary lines are 'drawn' on the Earth. Longitude lines run North-South between the poles. Latitude lines run horizontally around the Earth parallel to the equator.

Where these lines intersect gives a position like on the globe shown, this position is expressed in degrees either North or South of the equator and East or West of the Prime Meridian. The position on the globe is thus: 50° 00' .0 N, 030° 00' .0 W

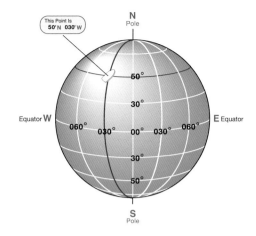

Each degree can be divided into fractions of a degree. Like hours, a degree consists of 60 minutes, and each minute consists of 60 seconds. Seconds are now usually expressed as decimals, so 42'30" becomes 42'.5.

On the globe, the craft is 50 degrees north (50°N); one degree of latitude equals 60 nautical miles, therefore since one minute of latitude equals one nautical mile (equals 1852m on land), in this example, 50° x 60 miles = 3000 miles North of the Equator.

A chart is only accurate on the day it is printed. Harbour authorities may move, add or remove buoys. Always check in the bottom left hand corner of the chart to see when it was last updated. Regular correction notices are published, and from these you should update your charts.

For chartwork we use plotting symbols to make things clear:

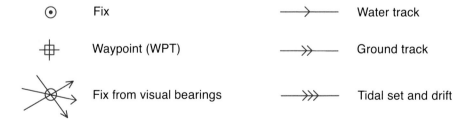

⊙   Fix

⟶   Water track

⊕   Waypoint (WPT)

⟹   Ground track

⊗   Fix from visual bearings

⟹⟩   Tidal set and drift

Measuring Distance on a Chart

When measuring distance, always take the dividers to the 'latitude' scale on the side of the chart alongside the area that you are measuring.

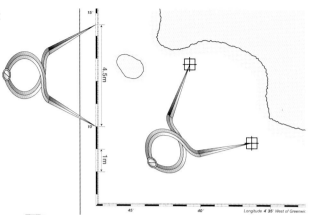

Plotting a Position

To plot a position on a chart from a latitude and longitude, mark off the latitude by marking a horizontal line in the rough area you expect it to intersect the meridian of longitude.

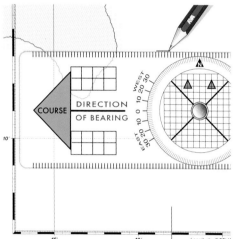

Then mark off the meridian of longitude from the scale at the top or bottom of the chart.

Where the lines intersect is the position.

When plotting you can either use a plotter or dividers. A plotter is easier on a small powerboat.

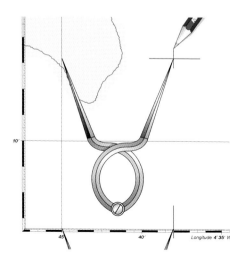

Tides

Tides are the changing depth of water above chart datum, more generally referred to as the vertical change in sea level - up and down. They are caused by the gravitational effect of the Moon and the Sun on the Earth and run roughly on a 28 day cycle with two 'Spring' and 'Neap' periods in each cycle.

Spring tides: when the Earth is in line with the Moon and Sun and the gravitational effect is at its greatest, this gives high tides at their highest, and low tides at their lowest.

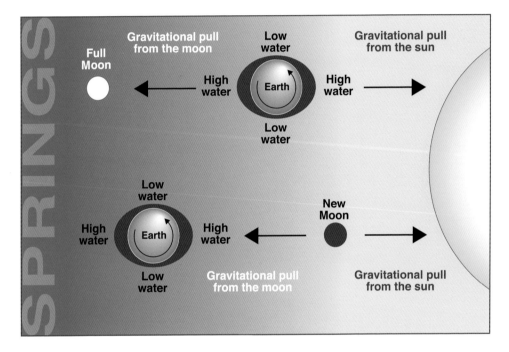

Neap tides: when the gravitational pull of the moon and the sun are split roughly at right angles the result is, the highs are less high and the lows are less low than at spring tides.

In between these extremes we have constantly changing value depending where we are in the cycle.

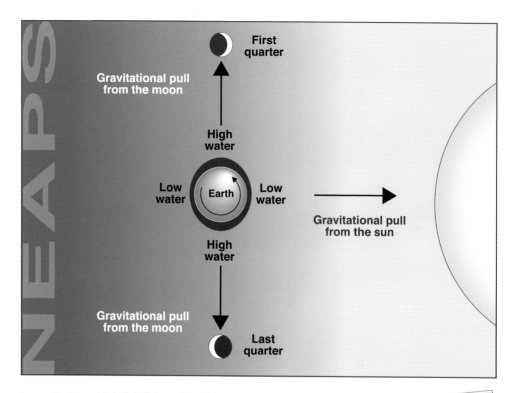

In most places high tide follows low tide on a roughly six hour cycle (i.e. two highs and two lows per day) and springs and neaps alternate on a seven day cycle.

Tidal information is available from a variety of sources – a nautical almanac, local tide tables or even the internet. Usually the times and heights of high and low water for the chosen port are given, sometimes there is also a tidal graph which gives more precise calculations.

Tidal Streams

Tidal streams are the movement of water as the tide floods and ebbs and as with springs we have a greater range of water (high tide higher and low tide lower) than with neaps it follows that the tide will flood and ebb faster at springs than neaps. This information is shown on charts (as tidal diamonds) and in tidal atlases and almanacs - usually both rate of flow and direction are shown. Knowing the rate and direction allows you to make a more informed decision for example:

A passage with the tide - will be faster and use less fuel

A passage with wind <u>against</u> tide - could be rougher

A passage with wind and tide <u>together</u> - may be smoother

Compass

To navigate at sea boaters use a compass, which allows you to steer on a particular heading, take bearings of known objects to plot your position and monitor the bearing to assess the risk of collision with other craft. Compasses point to Magnetic North. This is different from the chart which is aligned with True North. The difference between True and Magnetic North is called variation. If we are transferring bearings from a chart to use on a compass, they need to be converted from True to Magnetic. Likewise, when reading bearings from a compass they need converting to True before plotting on a chart. Variation can vary greatly between different boating areas, and changes over time. It is calculated and recorded on charts. Whilst afloat if we need to find our position and mark it on the chart, we can do this by using a three-point fix. This allows a position on the sea to be plotted onto a chart with reference to nearby land objects.

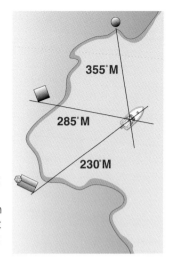

Electronic Navigation

The Global Positioning System (GPS) has now become the primary navigation system for small powerboats where space for chartwork is limited. When used in conjunction with a chart it makes progress along a pre-planned route easier. GPS systems show your current position and can also be programmed with waypoints (a position expressed in latitude and longitude). By entering a route using waypoints the GPS can show the bearing and distance from one waypoint to another.

GPS can also give your speed over the ground (SOG), course over the ground (COG) and show you how far you have strayed from your intended route (cross track error - XTE).

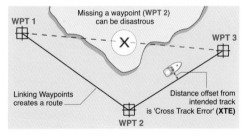

Buoyage

In IALA A (as shown below) we leave the starboard cone to our starboard side when entering harbour - our boat's port and starboard side match the buoyage. In IALA B the reverse is true.

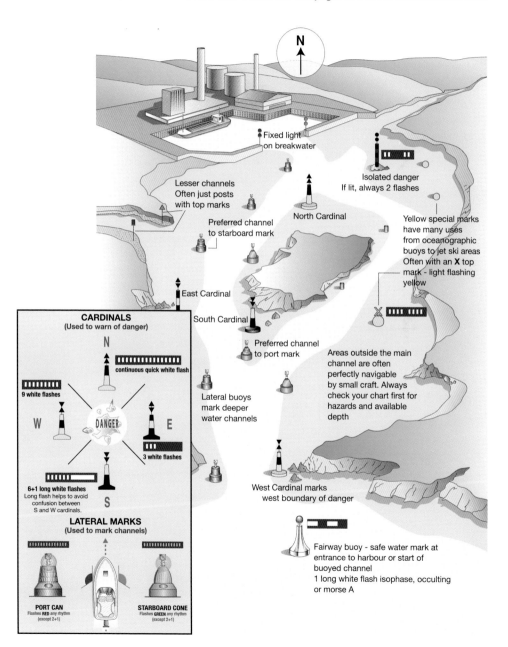

Fixed light on breakwater

Isolated danger
If lit, always 2 flashes

Lesser channels
Often just posts
with top marks

North Cardinal

Yellow special marks
have many uses
from oceanographic
buoys to jet ski areas
Often with an **X** top
mark - light flashing
yellow

Preferred channel
to starboard mark

East Cardinal

South Cardinal

Preferred channel
to port mark

Areas outside the main
channel are often
perfectly navigable
by small craft. Always
check your chart first for
hazards and available
depth

Lateral buoys
mark deeper
water channels

West Cardinal marks
west boundary of danger

Fairway buoy - safe water mark at
entrance to harbour or start of
buoyed channel
1 long white flash isophase, occulting
or morse A

CARDINALS
(Used to warn of danger)

N

continuous quick white flash

9 white flashes

W   DANGER   E

3 white flashes

6+1 long white flashes
Long flash helps to avoid
confusion between
S and W cardinals.

S

LATERAL MARKS
(Used to mark channels)

PORT CAN
Flashes **RED** any rhythm
(except 2+1)

STARBOARD CONE
Flashes **GREEN** any rhythm
(except 2+1)

Passage Planning and Pilotage

Passage planning is the ability to prepare a plan that allows you to safely navigate between two points. It will take into account: weather, stream, tidal rates, route, vessel and the experience of the crew. At the end of a passage you will use pilotage, which is the use of landmarks, buoyage, transits and water depth for departure and arrival at a known or unknown harbour or marina.

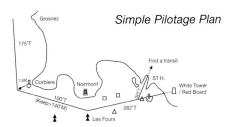

Simple Pilotage Plan

Weather

Weather information is available from television, radio, VHF, the internet and your local harbour or marina. A basic understanding of wind strength, direction and what effect it has while you are out on the water is essential for the skipper of a small boat. Remember wind against the stream will make the sea state worse (RYA Publication G133 RYA Weather Handbook).

The Beaufort Scale and Interpreting Weather Forecasts

Force	Wind Speed	Description	Wave Height	Sea State	What's it like?
0	< 1 knot	Calm	0m	Mirror-like	
1	1–3 knots	Light air	Up to 0.1m	Ripples on the surface	Ideal powerboating weather
2	4–6 knots	Light breeze	Up to 0.3m	Small wavelets with smooth crests	
3	7–10 knots	Gentle breeze	Up to 0.9m	Large wavelets with crests starting to break	
4	11–16 knots	Moderate breeze	Up to 1.5m	Large waves begin to form with white foam crests	Getting interesting
5	17–21 knots	Fresh breeze	Up to 2.5m	Moderate waves and many white horses	Only for the more experienced
6 >	21 knots >	Strong breeze +	2.5m +	Large waves +	Do something else!

Towing

When towing always make sure that the tow vessel is suitable in size for the task. Consider how far you will need to tow, ensure you have the correct lines and agree any charges before you start.

Astern Tow

An astern tow is usually the easiest tow for any distance. Agree a simple communications method before you start, use a long line which will act as a shock absorber, lead the tow line through any fairleads and spread the load on both craft over the strong points. It will be much easier to steer if the tow is from ahead of the outboard or rudder and on the centre line of the craft. Outboard powered craft can use a bridle for light tows. Adjust the tow length so that if there is any sea running you aim to use a line of twice the wavelength, to ensure that the vessel under tow sits comfortably on the waves coming behind you.

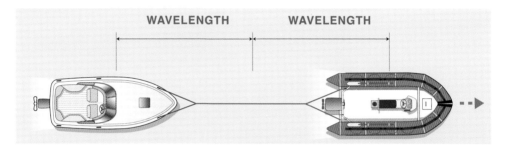

Towing Alongside

This is more like pushing the boat. Especially good when greater control is required - in harbour, or into a berth. The tow vessels must be toed-in slightly. The rudder or outboard of the towing vessel must be behind the towed vessel. Use the bow line to keep the vessels toed-in. The stern line holds it together when you turn corners. A tug's fore spring will take nearly all the weight when moving ahead. The tug's stern spring will take nearly all the weight when moving astern.

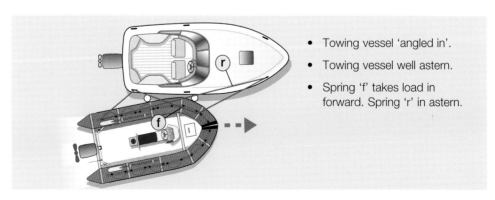

- Towing vessel 'angled in'.
- Towing vessel well astern.
- Spring 'f' takes load in forward. Spring 'r' in astern.

Glossary of Terms

Beaufort Scale	Scale of wind speeds.
Buoyancy aid	Similar to lifejacket, but less effective.
Cardinals	Compass orientated system for buoyage marking safe water.
Carrying away	Forward or reverse movement of craft whilst in neutral.
Cathedral hull	W shaped hull.
Cleat	Deck fitting for securing ropes.
Cone	Day shape identifying vessel type.
D-ring	Deck fitting for securing craft to trailer.
Diamond	Day shape identifying vessel type.
Displacement hull	Non-planning hull.
Dory hull	Fairly flat-bottomed hull.
Dry suit	Waterproof gear with more protection than wet suit.
Fairlead	Deck fitting for guiding ropes.
Freeboard	Vertical amount of hull above water.
GPS	Global Positioning System – satellite navigation system.
Give way vessel	Vessel obliged to keep clear of stand on vessel.
IALA	International Association of Marine Aids to Navigation and Lighthouse Authorities.
Jet drive	Propulsion and steering system using high pressure water.
Kill cord	Safety lanyard that cuts out engine in an emergency.
Lateral marks	Identification system for buoyage marking channels.
Leeward	Downwind direction/side.
MMSI	Unique craft identification number used with VHF DSC radio.
MOB	Man overboard.

Momentum	Forward or reverse movement of craft whilst in neutral.
Outdrive	Propulsion and steering system similar to outboard, but built into craft.
Painter	Mooring line attached to the boat.
Pivot point	Imaginary point around which the hull pivots when turning.
Planing hull	Hull type where its power allows it to rise on top of water at speed.
Plotter	Instrument used with navigation charts.
Prop effect	Transverse thrust of propeller.
RIB	Rigid Inflatable Boat.
Scope	Length of anchor chain and rope.
Semi-displacement hull	Part displacement, part Vee hull.
Shaft drive	Propulsion system using an inboard engine.
Spring	Mooring line restricting movement of craft fore and aft.
Stand on vessel	Vessel obliged to hold course and speed.
Stern drive	See Outdrive.
Stream	Effect of water movement.
Variation	Difference between True and Magnetic North.
Vee hull	Description of hull shape.
Warp	Rope, e.g. anchor warp.
Waypoint	Navigational position along route.
Windage	Amount of wind resistance offered by hull and superstructure.
XTE	Cross Track Error – distance offset from intended track when navigating.

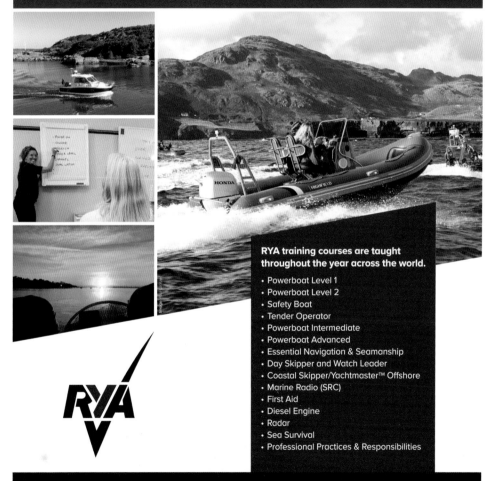

RYA Training Courses
FOR ALL AGES, ABILITIES AND ASPIRATIONS

Get the most from your time on the water with our range of practical, shorebased and online courses.

RYA training courses are taught throughout the year across the world.

- Powerboat Level 1
- Powerboat Level 2
- Safety Boat
- Tender Operator
- Powerboat Intermediate
- Powerboat Advanced
- Essential Navigation & Seamanship
- Day Skipper and Watch Leader
- Coastal Skipper/Yachtmaster™ Offshore
- Marine Radio (SRC)
- First Aid
- Diesel Engine
- Radar
- Sea Survival
- Professional Practices & Responsibilities

For further information visit **www.rya.org.uk/courses-training**, call **023 8060 4181**, or email **training@rya.org.uk**

WHY JOIN THE RYA?

OVER 80

RYA member
reward partners

Influencing policy on over
250 marine protected
areas in UK waters

Fighting for members'
rights on more than
20 Current Affairs topics

OnBoard has
introduced over

800,000

children to sailing

60,000+

disabled people have
been able to experience
sailing through the RYA
Sailability programme

Membership costs
from only

12p per day

2,500 international training
centres including the UK,
Australia, New Zealand,
South Africa, Indonesia,
Thailand and the USA

250,000

course completions
each year

OVER
815,000

visits to our Knowledge
and Advice web
pages a year

BUY ONLINE at

www.rya.org.uk/shop

Over 80 RYA books and eBooks to
support courses and expand knowledge

15%
DISCOUNT
for all RYA
members

eBooks

Many of our eBooks include animations,
videos and interactive tools to enhance learning.

There are multiple ways to buy eBooks.

Download the RYA Books App

Buy via Apple Books and Google Play

Find out more:
www.rya.org.uk/
go/ebooks